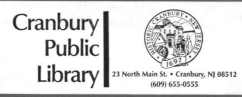

Bug Zone

Water

Bugs

Barbara Taylor

Chrysalis Education

US publication copyright © 2003 Chrysalis Education.
International copyright reserved in all countries.
No part of this book may be reproduced in any
form without written permission from the publisher.

Distributed in the United States by
Smart Apple Media
1980 Lookout Drive
North Mankato, MN 56003

Copyright © Chrysalis Books PLC 2003

ISBN 1-93233-311-8

Library of Congress Control Number 2003102441

Editorial manager: Joyce Bentley
Assistant editor: Clare Chambers

Project manager and editor: Penny Worms
Designer: Angie Allison
Picture researcher: Jenny Barlow
Consultant: Michael Chinery

Printed in Hong Kong

10 9 8 7 6 5 4 3 2 1

Words in bold can be found in the glossary on page 30.

All reasonable efforts have been made to trace the relevant copyright holders of the images contained within this book. If we were unable to reach you, please contact Chrysalis Education.

B = bottom; C = centre; L = left; R = right; T = top.
Front Cover Montage (main) RSPCA Photolibrary/Duncan I McEwan BL FLPA/Silvestris BCL FLPA/Foto Natura/J van Arkel BCR Papilio/Robert Pickett BR Warren Photographic/Kim Taylor Back Cover L RSPCA/Wild Images/Martin Dohrn R Papilio/Robert Pickett 1 (see cover) 4 (see cover) 5 RSPCA Photolibrary/Les Borg 6 (see cover) 7 FLPA/B. Casals 8 T Papilio/Robert Pickett B FLPA/B. Casals 9 T FLPA/Dembinsky PhotoAssociation B FLPA/B. Casals 10 (see cover) 11 FLPA/M. B. Withers 12 FLPA/B. Casals 13 Ecoscene/Williams 14 (see cover) 15 FLPA/Silvestris 16 OSF/ London Scientific Films 17 OSF/Alistair MacEwen 18 FLPA/FotoNatura/J van Arkel 19 Corbis/David A. Northcott 20 Corbis/Science Pictures Ltd 21 T FLPA/Silvestris B Papilio/Michael Maconachie 22 FLPA/Lynwood Chace 23 and 24 FLPA/Foto Natura/J van Arkel 25 RSPCA Photolibrary/Geoff du Feu 26 Papilio/Robert Pickett 27 (see cover) 28 Ecoscene/Kjell Sandved 29 Papilio/Alistair Shay.

Contents

Why do bugs live in water?

Some **bugs** live in ponds, lakes, and rivers because there is plenty of food to eat and they can easily escape from enemies.

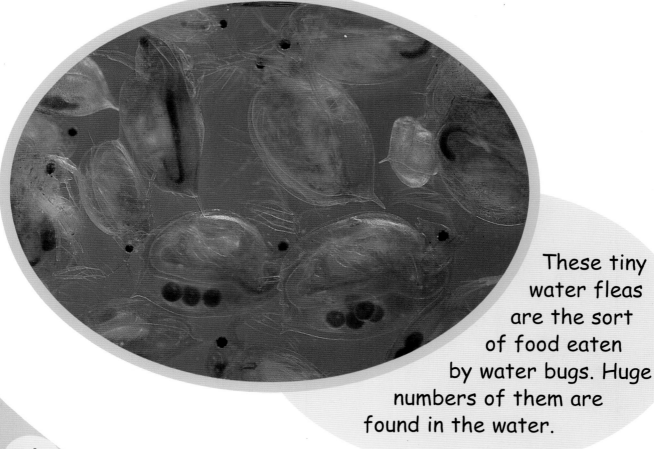

These tiny water fleas are the sort of food eaten by water bugs. Huge numbers of them are found in the water.

This **dragonfly** is laying eggs. Many bugs lay their eggs in water or on water plants and their young grow up in the water.

Water is a good place for bugs to protect their young. Not only are they hidden from many of their enemies, but they are protected from the weather.

Billions and billions of tiny water bugs drift on the surface of the sea. Some of the great whales eat them.

How do they breathe?

Great diving **beetles** collect air from the surface of the water and store it under their wing covers.

All living things need **oxygen** to survive. This includes water bugs, and they have developed different ways of getting the oxygen they need.

Some bugs go to the surface to breathe, like human swimmers. Some take oxygen down with them, like human divers. But the water is full of oxygen, and so some bugs take it from the water, like fish.

Pond snails can take air from the surface into a space inside their shell. They can also breathe underwater through their skin.

Feathery **gills** along the sides of this young **mayfly's** body help it to take in oxygen from the water.

Water babies

Mosquitoes have a **life cycle** that is typical of many water bugs. Their babies develop underwater. When they have grown into adults, they fly off into the air.

The female mosquito lays her eggs on the surface of the water. The eggs stick together to form a floating raft.

Baby mosquitoes, called **larvae**, hatch out of the trapdoors in the bottom of the eggs. They hang upside down from the water's surface by their breathing tubes.

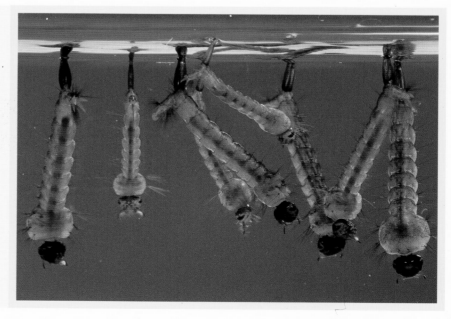

8

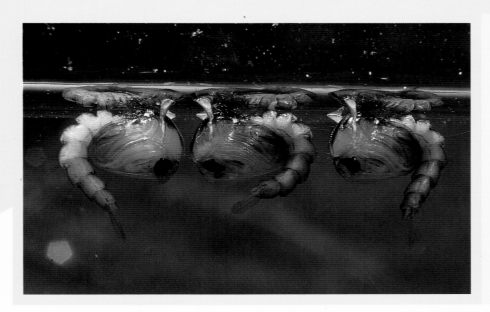

The larvae turn into **pupae**. Inside, the mosquito is changing into an adult.

The adult mosquito wriggles free. It is fully developed and can fly away.

Dreadful dragons

Can you see this nymph's long bottom lip? The nymph flips it out to spear **prey** with two spiky claws on the end.

Dragonfly babies are called **nymphs** and they are fierce underwater hunters.

Dragonflies take from one to three years to develop under the water.

Once a dragonfly nymph has changed into an adult, it cannot go back below the water or it will drown.

Adult dragonflies usually stay near the water. They zoom to and fro over the water like tiny helicopters, catching bugs to eat.

Clever caddis flies

Like dragonflies, adult **caddis flies** live in the air, while their young, or larvae, live under the water.

Adult caddis flies look rather like moths with hairy wings. They only come out at night.

The larvae build amazing cases for protection and **camouflage**. They hang onto their cases with hooks on the back of their bodies.

Caddis fly larvae live underwater for almost a year. The adults only live a few weeks.

The cases have a **silk** lining to which the larvae attach twigs, stones, shells, or sand.

13

Watery spiders

Fishing spiders use their legs to detect ripples on the water's surface made by prey. Then they skate out to grab a meal.

Fishing **spiders** float on the water's surface, often sitting on floating leaves or other objects. They wait for prey to come close and then they give chase.

The water spider is the only spider that spends its whole life underwater. To breathe, it builds a silk bubble and fills it with air from the surface.

This male spider is visiting a female in her bubble. Water spiders leave their bubbles to mate, catch food, or collect more air.

Water walkers

Very lightweight bugs can walk on the water's surface without breaking through it and sinking.

The water strider's long, thin legs spread out its weight. The water's surface bends under its feet like a trampoline but does not break.

This water cricket is feeding on a fly that has fallen onto the water and cannot fly away.

Lots of small creatures fall onto the water's surface and are trapped there. This means that there is plenty of food for bugs that can walk or skate over the water.

Water crickets are not crickets at all and don't even chirp! They are relatives of water striders.

Rowing boats

Water boatmen use their "beak" like a vacuum cleaner to suck up tiny plants and other food particles. They carry bubbles of air beneath their wings.

Two kinds of water bugs row themselves through the water using their long, flat back legs, which are like the oars on a rowing boat.

The water boatman swims the right way up while the backswimmer swims with its whole body upside down!

Backswimmers are fierce hunters with big appetites. They often attack creatures much larger than themselves, such as small fish.

Backswimmers carry their air supplies in a cage of hairs under the body. The air is lightweight so it makes the bugs flip upside down.

Water scorpions

Water **scorpions** are true water bugs. They spend most or all of their time underwater, only coming near the surface to take in air through a breathing tube.

Water scorpions may be as long as your finger.

Water scorpions have big, grasping front legs to catch prey, like real scorpions.

A water scorpion's breathing tube is like a **snorkel** sticking out of the back of its body.

There are two types of water scorpions— wide, flat ones and long, thin ones. The thin ones are also called needle bugs or water stick **insects**.

The breathing tube of the needle bug is almost as long as its body.

Beastly bugs

Giant water bugs and saucer bugs live underwater most of the time. Both take bubbles of oxygen down with them, trapped underneath their wings and between hairs under the body.

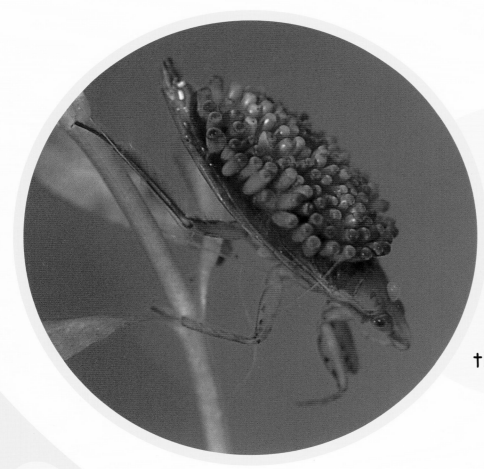

This male giant water bug carries eggs on his back, stuck there by the female. He carries them around until they hatch.

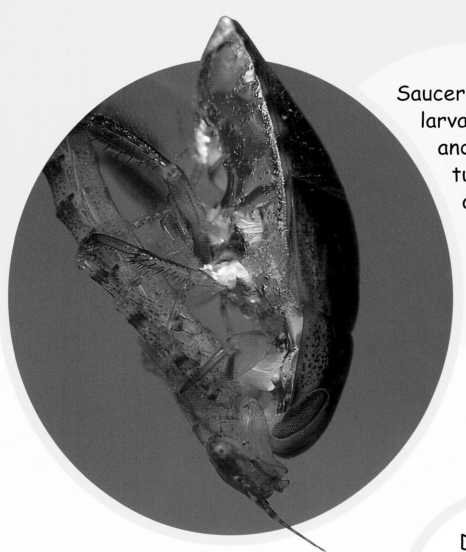

Saucer bugs catch larvae, water lice, and shrimps. They turn the insides of their prey into a sort of soup, before sucking it up.

Don't try to pick up a water bug or a saucer bug. They may give you a painful bite!

Both bugs are fierce hunters but giant water bugs are almost as big as a child's hand, while saucer bugs are only as long as a fingernail.

Fleas and lice

Water fleas and water lice live in fresh water but are related to the crabs and prawns that live in the sea. They are much smaller and more delicate than their sea relatives though.

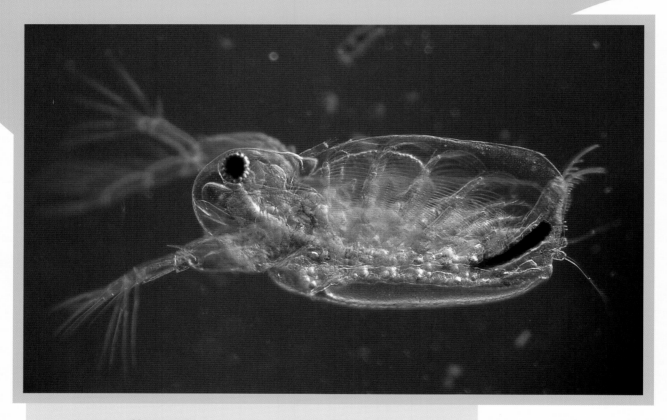

A water flea's body is see-through, which makes it hard to see. It looks the same color as the background.

The water louse is similar to the woodlouse. It has a flatter body so that fast-flowing water washes over it.

Water fleas are important because they are the first link in many **food chains**. Water lice are important because they clean up dead and decaying material by eating it.

If you have ever kept goldfish, you may have fed them dried water fleas!

Slippery snails

Pond snails lay their eggs in a mass of jelly, which protects the baby snails while they develop.

A snail's tongue, called a radula, has rows of tiny teeth. As the teeth wear down, new ones grow to replace them.

Like garden snails, water snails have a hard shell to protect their soft body. They can pull their body right inside the shell.

Most water snails feed on plants, scraping off bits of food with a rough tongue. They glide along on one big slimy foot.

The ramshorn snail has a shell coiled around like the horns of a ram, or male sheep.

Weird worms

Water worms live both in salty sea water and in fresh water. They take in oxygen from the water and do not need to come up for air.

Ragworms, have flat "legs," rather like paddles, with bristles on the end. These legs help them to move, but also take in oxygen from the water.

Tubifex worms live in groups at the bottom of ponds. They swallow mud and digest any small pieces of food in it.

Some water worms filter food from the water or mud, while others are hunters or feed on plants or dead material. A few—such as leeches—feed on animal blood.

King ragworms are usually about 8 in. long but may grow as long as 36 in. and be wider than a ruler!

Words to remember

beetle A flying insect with tough front wings that cover most of its body like a case.

breathing tube A thin tube rather like a straw, which some water bugs use to take in air from above the water.

bug A true bug is a type of insect with a stabbing beak. The word "bug" is now used to mean any type of minibeast.

caddis fly Adults are brown, flying insects with hairy wings. The young live in the water and many build cases.

camouflage Colors or patterns that blend in with the background.

dragonfly Adults are large hunting insects that fly well. The young are also hunters but live underwater.

food chain A series of feeding links, showing what animals eat.

gills A collection of thin flaps on a bug's body through which it takes in oxygen from the water.

insect A minibeast with three parts to its body and six legs. Most insects can fly.

larva A young insect that looks different from an adult. A larva is usually the feeding and growing stage in the life cycle. More than one larva are called larvae.

lifecycle The different stages in the life of a bug, including the egg, the young, and the adult.

mayfly Adults are delicate insects that live for just a few hours. They are weak fliers and live near water. The young live underwater and feed mainly on living and dead plants.

mosquito A type of fly. The females bite to feed on blood.

nymph A young insect that looks like an adult but is smaller and has no wings.

oxygen A gas in the air and in water, which all living things need to stay alive.

prey An animal that is killed or eaten by another animal.

pupa A resting stage in the life cycle of some insects, during which they change into their adult shape. More than one are called pupae.

scorpion A minibeast (not an insect), with two big claws and a powerful sting in its tail.

silk A fine, strong fiber produced by spiders and some insects.

snorkel A breathing tube used by swimmers near the surface of the water.

spider A minibeast (not an insect) with eight legs and two poisonous fangs.

Index